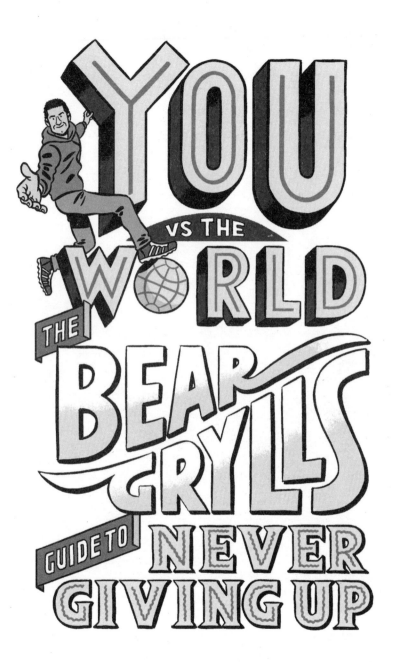

YOU
VS THE
WORLD
THE
BEAR
GRYLLS
GUIDE TO NEVER GIVING UP

CONTENTS

Hi there!

I'm **Bear Grylls,** and I'm going to help guide you on this epic adventure ahead! **I'm proud to have you on the team!**

I've been lucky to travel to some pretty incredible—and often unforgiving—places in my time, but none quite so challenging as the **big adventure** we call "life."

You see, as well as bringing us plenty of **good times and great things,** now and then, it might feel like the world really isn't on our side. It can often get tough and rough out there. Especially if we dream big!

But just like being prepared for an adventure, we can prepare ourselves for the tough stuff that might come our way in our lives. And by being smart, we can often **snatch success from the jaws of defeat!**

This book will **help you** do just that.

I like to think of it like packing a bag of gear for an expedition, but instead, we're packing a **bag full of handy tips and tricks** for dealing with conflicting emotions, physical obstacles, and mental challenges.

As we head out, I'll be **sharing many of my own stories** with you, so you can learn how I've done things—both rightly and wrongly! I am still learning just as much as you are.

So, are you ready to find out how to **survive and thrive** and to never give up, no matter what's going on in your life? Are you ready to harness YOUR adventurous spirit and climb YOUR Mount Everest?

Yes? Well then—what are we waiting for?
Let's do this!

CHAPTER 1

FIND FREEDOM

IN THE GREAT OUTDOORS

As a kid, I wasn't particularly brilliant at much at school. I was what would be called "average"! And I was also quite shy too. That meant that no one really noticed me much. **Which was fine.**

BUT ONE THING I ALWAYS LOVED WAS BEING OUTSIDE AS MUCH AS I COULD.

Whether it was scrambling up a steep hill with my dad, swimming in the sea, **climbing the tree** at the bottom of our garden, or just stomping in the puddles and playing with our dogs, all those things were fun for me. *And they felt natural.*

I GUESS I WAS "ABOVE AVERAGE" AT MESSING AROUND OUTSIDE, AND THE HOURS WOULD OFTEN SLIP BY.

ADVENTURES WITH DAD

I was lucky to have nature **right on my doorstep** for a good deal of my childhood. I lived in a small coastal town on the Isle of Wight, just off the south coast of England. **Being by the sea was brilliant,** even in winter. I loved watching the wild seas and big waves crashing in. They could be pretty intimidating.

It was as a young, quite introverted boy that I got my first sense of **the freedom of the outdoors.** The sort of freedom that comes from being **surrounded by nature** and from sometimes being challenged by its power. There are **fewer rules and regulations in wild spaces,** and I liked that.

Sometimes I wouldn't want to go outside if it was raining and cold, but **my dad would still encourage me** to go with him. After a few minutes of hiking, even if I was getting wet, I almost always realized **I was loving it.**

It's hard to explain. But simply being outside with my dad—breathing hard, climbing a hill, head down against the wind and rain—**somehow felt natural and good.**

IT'S WHERE MY LIFELONG **LOVE** OF THE OUTDOORS WAS BORN.

CLIMBING HIGH

Often when my dad and I set out on these adventures, we would make up a story about what we were doing. We weren't just climbing a steep hill—oh no!—**We were scaling Mount Everest,** and we could see the summit ahead.

If only we could somehow negotiate the ice field and crevasses in front of us. **He'd reach across with his stick, and I'd have to jump and grab it.**

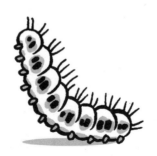

Sometimes we imagined that we were **silently sneaking up** on an enemy guard on sentry duty at this old derelict stone building that was halfway up the hill. **We had to be stealthy** and ready to pelt them with lumps of cow pat in order **to make it past safely!**

All this would fire up my imagination and made my time in the outdoors even more fun. I'll always be grateful to my late dad for that.

NATURE IS EVERYWHERE

It wasn't always easy to find open spaces, especially when I was back at school, or in London, where my dad worked. And often, I found it difficult to adjust to the rules and restrictions of life away from our island adventures. But I did my best to seek out adventure even in the city.

I climbed on the bike shed roofs and messed around in the park. The truth is, nature and adventure are often close at hand. We just have to look a little harder sometimes.

MY DAD USED TO SAY THAT ADVENTURE WAS REALLY A STATE OF MIND.

Next time you spot a butterfly or a squirrel, take a moment to stop and watch it moving. **So free. So in tune.** Move stealthily and see how close you can get. Or maybe go and touch a big tree in the park and look up into the branches. Just imagine how long it might have taken to get so big. **Some big trees are hundreds of years old.** All those years, fighting for light, water, and nutrients, and all the time, steadfastly watching the world go by.

Adventures can be found on a cliff face, but they can also be found in cities or other urban areas. **In truth, nature is often closer to us than we might imagine.**

Take time to stop and quietly observe, whether that means noticing a thriving weed squeezing out from the pavement or a bird soaring above our heads. Scientists have found that being connected to the natural world is **SO important** for our health. It allows our brains to slow down and takes us away from our screens and the demands of life. Nature always heals us.

Sometimes it can take a lifetime to understand this. But start now. Get outside and lie on the grass. Listen, connect, observe. **And interact.** Nature is a gift to us all.

CHAPTER 2

IT'S OK TO BE AFRAID;

IT'S WHAT YOU DO NEXT THAT COUNTS

People sometimes say to me: **"I bet you're not scared of anything."** But nothing could be further from the truth. I know exactly what it's like to be afraid.

Fear is totally normal and isn't always a bad thing. It's good for alerting us to potential DANGER. But if we are a slave to our fears, that can also stop us from achieving our dreams.

There are ways that we can take our fear and **turn it into something hugely positive.** I've finally learned how to do this in my life, and you can do it in yours.

I couldn't tell you how many times I have felt that queasy sensation of terror deep in the pit of my stomach. That feeling is all too familiar to me. When your brain says: **"Nuh-huh, not for me thanks, bye"** and pulls its shutters down with a loud bang.

YOU KNOW IT?

You might even go cold or get jittery. That's something called an **adrenaline rush.** It's thanks to a substance called adrenaline that is released in your body when you're frightened about something. **It gets our body ready to stand and fight** the scary thing or to avoid conflict and run away at top speed—whichever decision is smartest.

But adrenaline can also make it hard to think or make good choices if you're not used to the sensation.

That's why I don't avoid scary things.
Instead, I want to be familiar with that feeling of adrenaline and know how to handle it.

I WANT THAT ADRENALINE TO WORK FOR ME, NOT TO CONTROL OR OVERWHELM ME.

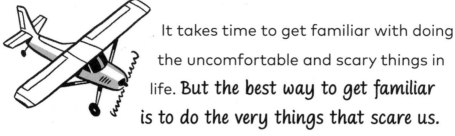

It takes time to get familiar with doing the uncomfortable and scary things in life. **But the best way to get familiar is to do the very things that scare us.**

Because when we move toward the things we fear, we learn that those things aren't always so frightening after all. That's how we can then achieve amazing things.

Each and every time we face something difficult and move toward it, our ability to deal with fear gets stronger, and we get smarter. That's what courage is.

COMING BACK FROM A BROKEN BACK

If there is a nightmare scenario you never want to come true, it's your parachute failing during a skydive, right? **Well, that nightmare happened to me.**

I was around 21 years old and working in southern Africa for the summer. Skydiving was what we did for fun on our days off. Trust me, there's nothing like the feeling of total freedom as you drop from an airplane and fall through the sky. I loved that feeling of being 14,000 feet **above the ground.**

Then, on one skydive with my friends, **my parachute failed** to open properly. I didn't manage to get my reserve chute open in time, and I ended up hitting the dusty desert floor at high speed. My back was broken in three places. **It felt like all my hopes and dreams for the future had been shattered along with my spine.**

I WAS TERRIFIED FOR MY FUTURE.

I had to spend many months in recovery and rehab, not knowing if I would be able to walk properly again, let alone do the job in the **British Special Forces** that I had trained so hard to win.

But during this dark, scary time, I learned that if I wanted to get back on my feet and follow my dreams, I would have to face many scary moments ahead. Many battles in my head—battles of confidence and nerves—as much as battling the physical pain in my back. **It's about doing whatever it takes,** despite the fear, so we can live a life that we are excited by and are proud of.

JUST JUMP!

Believe it or not—and you'll probably already know this if you've seen any of my TV shows—I have

skydived many, many times since that accident. I've jumped from pretty much every sort of aircraft you can think of—**helicopters, hot-air balloons, old World War II planes, and even off cliffs.**

I wonder if you know this too: Every time I jump, **I still feel so much fear.** I can't sleep that well the night before. At times, I still have nightmares about falling out of control. That full-on, sweaty-palmed, stomach-churning, nauseous terror. But if I want to do the job I love to the best of my ability, I have to force myself to face that fear and do it anyway. **And then I love it.**

Because here's what I've learned: The more we face the difficult stuff, and the more we **refuse to run** from our fears, the better we become at overcoming them.

BREAKING RECORDS

I would have lost out on so many **incredible** opportunities if I had let my fear of skydiving get the better of me. But there's one in particular that I'm so glad I didn't miss. **It always makes me smile** to think about it.

In 2005, **suspended beneath a hot-air balloon** flying at a whopping 25,000 feet above the ground, a friend and I held the world's highest open-air formal dinner party.

Between gasps of oxygen, we sat at a tiny table hanging below the basket on long wires, and we dined on a three-course meal, dressed in our formal Navy uniforms. **Then we dropped off and skydived to Earth.**

The feat had taken us two years to plan, and it earned us an entry in **The Guinness World Records.** Most importantly, it helped support an amazing UK charity called The Duke of Edinburgh's Award that helps young people develop skills for life.

If I'd been too afraid to skydive again after my accident, I would have missed out on this once-in-a-lifetime moment *and* on the chance to become a **world record holder** with a great buddy of mine.

POTATOES OR PLAYING CHESS

Of course, you don't need to be aiming for world records in order to face your fears. It's more about developing a **champion's state of mind.** It's about not running away from our natural fears but learning to harness them so that they actually help us **be our best.**

What's going on in your life that makes you feel afraid? Are you about to start a new school and you're afraid you won't make friends? Or perhaps you're holding yourself back from trying out for the chess club because you're afraid of losing a match?

It doesn't matter if you're eating potatoes at 25,000 feet above Earth after breaking your back or facing your opponent over a chess board. Real courage is about looking your fear straight in the eye and saying: "I'm going to do it anyway."

So don't be afraid to be afraid. Instead, make fear your friend, and use it to keep you sharp and to help you achieve your goals. You've really got nothing to lose.

YOU'VE GOT THIS. SO LET'S GO FOR IT!

CHAPTER 3

THE LIFE-CHANGING

MAGIC OF
NGU

Have you ever been in a tough situation where you just thought: "That's it. I can't go on"? I bet you have. Those moments can be really hard. But they are also an opportunity, because they give us the chance to decide how we respond.

WILL WE GIVE IN, OR DO WE GIVE MORE?

I've been in those sorts of tricky moments quite a few times, and they are not easy. They demand that we do something difficult and testing. To hold on a little bit longer.

TO KEEP GOING.
TO NEVER GIVE UP.

Even when we don't feel at all capable or strong.

That takes something special. And it often means making that conscious decision to **embrace the difficult** and choose the challenging. Many people throw in the towel at this point.

BUT IF YOU CAN KEEP GOING A LITTLE BIT LONGER, YOU HAVE A CHANCE TO ACHIEVE SOMETHING AMAZING.

To never give up takes courage and commitment. But it is always worth it.

When most people give up, we can choose to make that a trigger **to give more.**

As you might have guessed from the title of this book, "never give up" is something I really believe in! In fact, it has now become simply "NGU" in my family. But making the decision to not give up takes an inner strength that doesn't just appear overnight. It's something that grows in you the more you encounter tough times. And that's good news, because it means **the ability to never give up is like a muscle.**

THE MORE WE USE IT, THE STRONGER IT GETS.

That's why it's good to look for opportunities to build that muscle. Look for difficult things. Big challenges. Things that scare you. Fail at them, but get back up and try again. And boom! You're now training your all-important NGU muscle.

DREAMING OF A MOUNTAIN

Ever since I was a little kid, I had a dream. My dad and I talked about it endlessly when we were on our outdoor adventures together. He even gave me a picture for my bedroom wall to remind me of it. **The dream was to climb the HIGHEST mountain in the world: Mount Everest.**

I grew older, but the dream never left me. After I left school, I traveled in India, where **I saw the mighty Everest with my own eyes from many miles away.**

IT WAS AWESOME. HUGE AND TERRIFYING, EVEN ON THE DISTANT HORIZON.

I bought a bigger version of the picture my dad had given me—poster-sized this time—and I vowed there and then to do everything I could to make my dream of climbing the mountain a reality, **even though I didn't really know what it would entail.**

Life went on. I joined the British Army, and during that time, I had my bad skydiving accident and broke my back in three places.

I had to be in a military rehabilitation center to try and recover. I lay in my bed not knowing if I would ever be able to walk again and looking up at the picture of Everest that I still had on my wall. That dream felt a long way away.

BUT IN THE END, IT WAS THAT MOUNTAIN THAT BECAME THE CENTER OF MY RECOVERY. IT GAVE ME A GOAL AND A TARGET TO GET STRONG AGAIN FOR.

I never gave up on my Everest dream, and 18 months after my accident, I finally got to stand on the summit of the **biggest, baddest mountain in the world.**

TWO STEPS FORWARD, ONE STEP BACK

There were so many NGU moments during my recovery and during the long, three-month Everest expedition itself. But each time, I treated those moments as a test: Would I give more, or would I give up? **"Choose to give more. Keep going. NGU."**

Because whether we're climbing a HUGE mountain at extreme altitude or tackling tough moments in everyday life, at times, we all need that NGU attitude. Sometimes, we will have to take two steps forward, then we will experience a setback. **Life is like that.** There will always be obstacles on the way to our goals and our summits. That's normal.

When climbing Everest, climbers can't just head straight to the summit. **Their body couldn't handle the thin air.** Instead, they have to climb up as high as possible and then descend back down to allow their body to adjust before going back up once more. **Each time higher, farther,** slowly adjusting to the oxygen-starved air.

Climbers eventually end up climbing the mountain almost five times in the process of going up and down. Just like life. **Win. Lose. Fall down. Get up.** But all the time, bit by bit, we get closer and closer to standing on top of the world. Just never give up. **The rewards will be waiting for you at the top.**

GETTING TO THE GOOD STUFF

NGU is the most important tool in our backpack for handling the difficult things in life. **It's also the key to unlocking the really cool stuff.** If we want to reach the top in anything—whatever that might be—then start training that NGU muscle right now. **Remember: aim big, fail often, get back up, and NGU.**

WHAT'S YOUR MOUNT EVEREST?

HAVE YOU GOT A DREAM YOU WOULD DO ANYTHING TO ACHIEVE?

CHAPTER 4

TAKE A DEEP BREATH

AND
DO IT!

The twenty-sixth president of the United States of America, Theodore Roosevelt, once said: "Believe you can, and you're halfway there." It's a true and inspiring quote for sure, but I also know from experience that it isn't always easy to **believe in yourself.**

If you struggle with your confidence, you are not alone. I've been there. Often.

CONFIDENCE IS SOMETHING WE BUILD RATHER THAN FIND

The first big break that I ever got after I left the military was when a TV producer read about my Everest climb and contacted me and offered me the chance to do a TV show in America. It was a huge break and a generous offer, but I just didn't feel confident that I could do it.

Foolishly, I said no to him—not just once but three times.

Eventually, it was my wife Shara—we'd just gotten married at this stage—who suggested that maybe I should **give it a go.** After all, it would be good work, and I needed to earn us money.

Looking back, I had been wrong to turn down the producer's offer initially. But when we lack confidence and **belief in our own abilities**, it can be hard to go for things that intimidate us, even when we know that they are great opportunities.

Luckily, the producer hadn't given up, and when he came to me for a fourth time, **I nervously said yes.**

Even though that first US TV series felt a bit rough and ready—**I was trying to learn how to do the TV side of things while on the job!**—the series turned out alright. Yet I still struggled with being in front of the camera. It felt so weird to me. It felt like everyone was watching me just to pick holes in what I was doing.

Often when we most need confidence, it can be hardest to find. Despite not feeling very confident, I decided that I would keep learning, saying yes, giving my all, and then

SEE WHERE IT MIGHT LEAD.

The strange thing about confidence is that if we are determined, do our best, and try not to think about ourselves too much, then often the confidence sneaks up on us. **And suddenly it is there.**

But most people don't do the first part—the doing their best even when they feel unsure of themselves bit—and that's why they often don't get to experience the confidence at the end.

Real confidence is quiet and is all about what's going on inside us. But confidence is also like a muscle. And when we are determined and go for it, despite the fears, then that **confidence muscle gets stronger.**

TAKE A STAND AGAINST DOUBT

Doubt is something we will always experience, no matter how confident we might be. Doubt is part of life. It's a natural part of being a little nervous about what is ahead. And a bit of **doubt and nerves** are not always a bad thing.

Doubt is all about what we do with it. Do we let it stop us, or do we use it to drive us?

I like to look at doubts as obstacles and challenges to be overcome. Yes, I feel nervous, and yes, I'm unsure about what will happen, and yes, I might fail. But without those challenges, there is no adventure. It is when we go for things—despite the doubts—**that the real adventure begins!**

Dealing with doubt is all about whether we listen to it or whether we use it.

Like when **I was full of doubt** about my ability to do the TV series. Those feelings were natural. But when I decided to go for it and do it to the  best of my ability, then my confidence grew, and the doubts faded.

Of course, I still have moments during filming today when **I have to work hard to find my confidence** and banish the doubts, but I now realize that's all part of the adventure.

I will never forget standing on an Alaskan glacier, waiting for Barack Obama to arrive for an adventure with me. **I kept thinking, "How did this happen?!"** But then I told myself: "You've got this, Bear. Just do your best." And

as soon as the former president emerged from the trees in front of me, **I took a slow breath and just went for it.**

Barack Obama has since said that it was one of the **best days of his whole presidency.** That made us all feel pretty good and proud that we had said yes and committed to **do our best.**

EVERYONE'S FIGHTING THEIR OWN BATTLE

As you now know, in my early TV days, I wasted a lot of time **worrying about what other people thought.** Was I not very good at my job? Was there someone who could be doing it better?

But here's the truth of it: Most of the time, other people are more preoccupied with battling their own doubts and fears than with thinking about us. So we don't need to worry about other people's opinions of us. Let them be. What matters is **our journey,** staying in the arena, and giving our all.

The late basketball legend Kobe Bryant said: **"Nobody criticizes good—only great."** So when people do have an opinion about how you are doing, know that you're out there making things happen. It's a compliment!

And I love this quote: *"Don't worry about the opinion of someone you wouldn't take advice from."* That makes it all much simpler!

CONFIDENCE WILL COME

As Chief Scout, I love seeing young Scouts *grow in confidence* as they learn new skills and enjoy new experiences. Learning new things empowers us to be better and do better, **and I don't just mean school learning.**

The truth is, whenever we find something hard and yet we do it, *that's a real school day.* That's how we really learn and **grow** *and get stronger.*

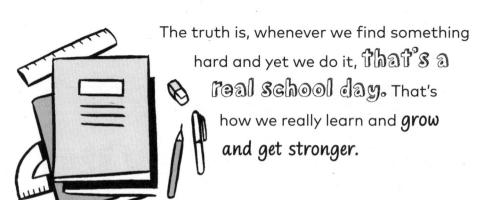

I remember the first time I learned how to cook a sausage using just one match. (Top tip: You have to use the match to light a fire, rather than trying to keep the single match lit long enough to cook the sausage!) I was a short, scrawny little six-year-old Scout. I was intimidated by all the bigger boys and **not really sure what I was doing.**

But I was **determined to give new things a try,** even if a lack of confidence made that difficult at times. But as I grew in **skill and experience,** my confidence grew too. And that's how all great journeys begin.

As President Theodore Roosevelt also said: **"Do what you can, with what you have, where you are."**

DO THAT, AND THE REST WILL FOLLOW.

CHAPTER 5

KINDNESS
MAKES

THE
WORLD
GO ROUND

Can you guess what type of person is the best to go on an expedition with? **The toughest? The strongest? The bravest?** These are all good qualities, and they for sure matter on a trip into the wild. But there's one quality that trumps all of these. **Can you guess what that might be?** Clue: It's often underrated by people in life. That is, until they receive or need it.

It's something that's in all of us. We've just got to make the decision to break it out every single day and use it as much as we can.

YOU'VE GOT IT.

IT'S KINDNESS.

THE LAST DROP

There was one time when I received an act of kindness in a desperate situation, and I will never forget it. I was out on an SAS patrol in the north African desert. Our helicopter was delayed by two days in coming to get us. **We each had one bottle of water left.** That meant one tiny sip every hour. We were seriously dehydrated and getting weaker by the hour. It didn't help that I was also suffering with diarrhea, and heatstroke was closing in on us all. **We were in trouble.**

Finally, we got the news that the helicopter would be picking us up 20 miles away **across the desert.**

Would we have the strength to cover that distance in our dehydrated state?

We were a small band of pretty hardened soldiers, but even so, **it would be a monumental struggle** to complete that distance. Especially with diarrhea.

I didn't know how—or even if—I was going to manage it.

Halfway into the trek, Sergeant Chris Carter—the leader of our patrol—could see **I was really struggling.** He also knew how to fix it... **at a MAJOR cost to himself.**

He only had one capful of water left in his bottle, but **Sergeant Carter gave that final capful to me.** He didn't make a big deal of it to the rest of the team. In fact, no one else even saw it. He just made me drink it, **even though he was totally parched himself.**

Sergeant Carter's kindness—**not the water**—was the true motivation that drove me on. He had my back, and so I would have his. **We pushed forward as a team, and together, we made it.**

HIS KINDNESS CHANGED EVERYTHING FOR ME. KINDNESS DOES THAT TO PEOPLE.

TIME IS PRECIOUS... SO GIVE IT AWAY!

Kindness doesn't always have to be things or money. It can simply be **showing someone you care** by giving them a hug or texting them something nice. What about if someone's having a hard time at home or at school **and could use a friend to hang out with?**

Mother Teresa was a nun who spent her whole life caring for the poor and the sick. She helped so many people by being kind. She once said: **"Help one person at a time, and always start with the person nearest you."**

Who might be **grateful for some kindness today?** Does someone need help reaching something on a grocery store shelf? Or a smile as you pass by? Maybe you could hold the door open for someone coming through behind you. **Little things like this don't cost us much, but they can make a huge difference to someone else.** And like with Sergeant Carter, we never forget.

INSPIRATION AND MOTIVATION

It's always inspiring when we see others being kind. I definitely feel motivated to be kinder when I see young Scouts sitting beside people suffering with dementia. **The young people hold their hands.** They chat with them. These brilliant Scouts take the time to care. They could be off doing any number of other things—and often are!—but they make time to do something kind. **Kindness changes everything for the better,** whatever the situation you're in.

IT MAKES US ALL BETTER

The brilliant thing about being kind is that it also makes the person who gives it happy. That's why Mother Teresa had a face that people used to say **shone like the sun.** She spent her whole life giving.

It's a true fact of life: When we give something away, we receive even more back in return. It is like a boomerang. We receive happiness, peace, and the love, admiration, and gratitude of others. **Because how you treat others really can affect how they treat you.**

WHEN PEOPLE THINK OF YOU, DO YOU WANT THEM TO THINK OF YOU AS A KIND PERSON?

I DO.

IT'S THE KING OF QUALITIES.

CHAPTER 6

TRUST THE

VOICE INSIDE

Have you ever had that sense, deep down inside, that you know something is right, but you can't explain why or how you  know? Like if you ask someone a question, and you just know that their reply isn't the truth? Some people call that instinct. Others might call it intuition or a gut feeling. Whatever we choose to call it, it's a powerful thing coming from deep inside our heart, and we should use it to help us in life as much as we can.

OUR SECRET WEAPON

The good old dictionary tells us that instinct is "a natural ability that helps us decide what to do or how to act without thinking." It's not something we learn, and it can't be changed by someone else's opinions or actions. It's ours, built into who we are. Pretty cool, huh?

Even so, some people choose to ignore this Secret weapon because they are in too much of a rush or are too stubborn to realize that it can be of enormous use to them.

But, as the **smartest adventurers** will tell you, instinct is the special sauce on top of all their skill, training, and strength.

IT'S THAT UNIQUE INGREDIENT THAT WILL CARRY THEM THAT FINAL STEP TO THE SUMMIT OR OVER THE FINISH LINE.

It's like the nose of your mind. It can smell the right thing to do.

GETTING LOST IN THE MOUNTAINS

The first time I came across my own little voice inside, I was 11 years old, and I was on a family trip to visit my uncle in Cyprus. He was an army officer out there, and he suggested that **we could go to the local ski slope in the mountains.**

After a few hours of going up and down this one ski run, my dad and I made a spontaneous decision to go and ski off-piste. We thought that we'd very quickly **explore the forest** beyond the recognized ski route.

Turns out there was nothing quick about it. Before long, the mist rolled in, and we found ourselves **utterly and completely lost.** Not good. We had made a BIG mistake going off-piste with no plan, no knowledge of the area, and no map. **(But we all make mistakes from time to time.)**

Not only did we have no map or compass, **but we had no food or drink.**

AND THIS WAS IN THE DAYS BEFORE CELL PHONES—IF YOU CAN BELIEVE IT—SO NO PHONE.

We had no choice but to trudge on, us getting colder, the snow getting deeper, and the day getting darker.

Eventually, we came to a fork in the valley. There were two options: right or left? I was so tired and freezing cold, but I was also aware of a very strong sense—deep in my gut and cutting through all the exhaustion—that the left fork was the way to go. In my bedraggled state, I could easily have given in when Dad said that we should maybe go right, **but I didn't.**

SOMETHING WAS TELLING ME WE NEEDED TO GO LEFT, AND I KNEW I HAD TO LISTEN.

We took the left fork and soon afterward, **as if by some miracle,** we found a small track to follow. It quickly led us to a road where we hitched a ride in a car going back up the mountain to safety! **Who knows if we'd have made it out alive** in those conditions if we had gone right?

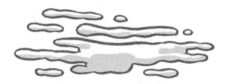

Of course, the happy ending to this story could be seen as **just luck,** but one thing I know for certain is that I heard that voice inside me urging me to take the left fork, and I took notice of it.
I listened.

I had no idea how that voice could be so sure. I had never even been to Cyprus before, let alone to that precise area.

But there was something taking over the logical, thinking part of my brain and saying: "Just trust me, Bear. I'm telling you, the left fork is the one!" **And that inner voice was right.**

GETTING INTO TROUBLE!

By the way, not everyone was as happy as we were when we staggered back into the army barracks in the early hours of the morning. My dad and I were both so happy and relieved at

surviving our adventure, but my uncle wasn't so upbeat. He was looking very serious. He then told us that **he had mobilized the entire army mountain rescue team** to search for us, helicopters and all. He thought that we had been foolish and reckless. He was probably right.

The point is, after this experience in the mountains, **the more I listened to my instinct when it spoke to me,** the better I became at trusting it and letting it guide me, even though I couldn't explain it in any sort of logical way.

Our little voice inside is there to help us. And while it won't always guide us to the easier path, it will guide us to the RIGHT one. **Trust it when it speaks— your heart will never lie.**

CHAPTER 7

TEAMWORK MAKES THE

DREAM
WORK

Have you ever heard an adult say: "There's no 'I' in team"? T-E-A-M... **Nope, definitely no "I" to be found!** It's a bit of a cheesy catchphrase, but it's something that is so true. All the great teams that perform spectacularly—whether on a mountain or on a football field—are made up of people who put the team before themselves. They don't seek glory, or approval, or rewards only for themselves; they prefer to win those things for the team. **And it's amazing to see.**

Great teams have each other's backs no matter what. They start their sentences with "we" instead of "I." **We're** going to win the match. **We'll** make it to the summit. **We will be okay.**

SUCCESS IS GREATEST WHEN SHARED

There's an African proverb that says: "If you want to go fast, go alone. If you want to go far, go together." It's so true, but it isn't always easy. Being a real team player sometimes means allowing others to shine instead of ourselves.

But when we do things as a team and put our teammates' interests ahead of our own, the success is all the sweeter. When all the team members work together in sync, the results are so much better than anything we could ever do alone.

SUCCESS ON OUR OWN CAN BE LONELY. SUCCESS AS A TEAM IS EXHILARATING.

THREE TEAMWORK TIPS

The best teams always apply three simple rules when working together. If we try to remember these, then we're already on course to succeed!

1) A UNIQUE ROLE

Make sure that **everyone** on the team has a role that is theirs. It should reflect what they are best at. Then, make sure that everyone knows each other's role.

2) A SHARED GOAL

Speaking of goals, we want to make sure that everyone in the team knows what the **ultimate goal** is and agrees on what that goal should be. Keep it simple. Keep it clear.

This is something to be 100% certain of before we start.

3) HELP OTHERS SHINE

It's the great secret to great teams: When we help our **teammates** do well and shine, that's when the team is most likely to win. It's not just those who score the goals who make the real difference, but those who set them up.

Be a setter-upper, and your team will thrive.

BUILD A TEAM ON FRIENDSHIP

I've had the privilege of being part of **many unique teams** in my life. In order to reach the summit of Everest, I climbed as part of a team. Working as a soldier in the Special Forces, I was part of a team. And in my television work, even though I'm the one you see on screen, **I am just one part of a team** of people whose roles are equally as important as mine.

Each team was working toward different goals, but there was one thing in common—everyone behaved like a friend to each other, even when times were really hard. **Be a friend in times of need.**

In all of these teams, **we faced real fear,** long treks, extreme temperatures, heavy packs, and many critical moments, but the great team members always did everything they could to keep everyone going and to encourage the team to shine. That's teamwork, and it's also leadership. **The two go hand in hand.**

If someone is lower on energy than others and needs more food than they have in their rations, **great team members share.** They make each other laugh when someone wants to cry. **They help each other stand when some feel like collapsing.**

As the saying goes: "Iron sharpens iron." If we are all being the best teammates we can be—**"doing our best,"** as the Scouts say—then we will sharpen each other, and **we will help each other be the best we can be.**

THAT'S HOW YOU WIN.

CHAPTER 8

AN ATTITUDE

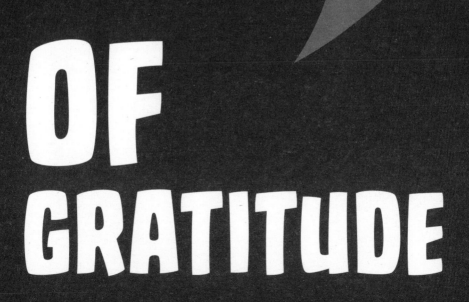

OF
GRATITUDE

What if I told you that there was something you could do every day that was quick, simple, and might help you live a happier life? **It's called gratitude,** or being thankful, and we can practice it like we would a sport or a musical instrument.

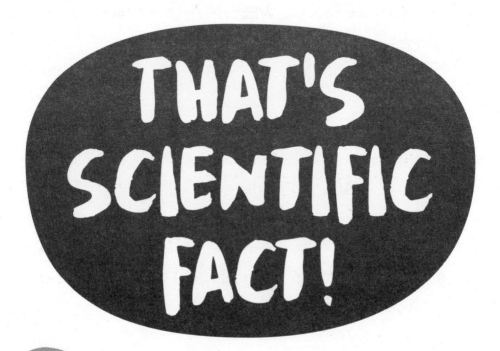

BRAIN TRAINING

Incredible things happen in our bodies when we practice gratitude and say thank you for the many simple, good things in our lives. When we take time to slow down and think about the things that we are grateful for, **chemicals are released in our brains** that are designed to make us feel good.

THAT'S SCIENTIFIC FACT!

Human nature often focuses on the negative rather than the positive, and part of that is thanks to our prehistoric ancestors. They were always alert to danger and anticipating threats **that might mean the difference between life and death.** But as humans have evolved, we have developed the ability to choose what we focus on. So, if there is no imminent danger around, we can choose to focus on the good stuff rather than the bad!

PRACTICE HAPPY!

You're probably saying: **"OK, Bear, but how do I do this gratitude thing?"** Well, here's one way to think about it: What do we do to get better at anything? We do it over and over again.

The more we practice gratitude, the more we can train our brain to focus on the good stuff in our life instead of focusing on what isn't so good.

And that's always smart.

Skateboarding tricks, dance moves, penalty kicks. **We can build gratitude into our daily routine** in a similar way—it doesn't take up much time.

We could try to start every day by thinking of a couple of things **we're grateful for,** perhaps while we're brushing our teeth. Maybe it's gratitude that we get to see our friends at school. **Or that we've got a tasty breakfast to enjoy.** We can practice gratitude in the evening too, while we're getting ready for bed.

Try and think of a couple of things that have happened in your day that **you are grateful for.**

DID SOMEONE HELP YOU WITH SOMETHING?

DID SOMEONE CHEER YOU UP WITH A SMILE?

DID YOU SEE SOMETHING THAT MADE YOU HAPPY?

BEING GRATEFUL FOR LIFE

Sometimes, bad things happen to us unexpectedly. **That's just life.** But those tough things can also give us **opportunities to be grateful.**

I can think of one time that made me **very grateful just to be alive.** It was during the Everest expedition I was part of, and after an exhausting day of climbing, I was descending through this huge glacier. I took one step, and an enormous crack in the ice opened up beneath my feet **without warning.**

I WENT PLUNGING INTO THE DARKNESS. THEN, SUDDENLY, I WAS SWINGING ON THE END OF MY ROPE.

I had attached myself to that rope only seconds before I fell. **(Those few seconds saved my life.)** But still, here I was, hanging by only the thinnest of climbing ropes that could break at any point. The dark wall of ice around me was smooth and glassy, and I **couldn't get a proper hold** to try to haul myself up. All I could see beneath me was **never-ending darkness.**

I THOUGHT I WAS ABOUT TO DIE.

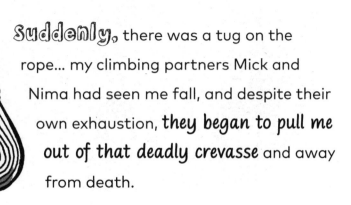

Suddenly, there was a tug on the rope... my climbing partners Mick and Nima had seen me fall, and despite their own exhaustion, **they began to pull me out of that deadly crevasse** and away from death.

That night, when I crawled back into my tent, utterly drained and still shaken, I wrote these words in my journal:

I DON'T THINK I HAVE EVER FELT SO CLOSE TO BEING KILLED AS I DID TODAY... IT LEAVES ME WITH THIS DEEP GRATITUDE FOR ALL THE GOOD AND BEAUTIFUL THINGS IN MY LIFE.

Luckily, we don't have to be close to death to be able to practice being grateful! Gratitude is a state of mind. A way to live. And being grateful makes every situation a little bit better.

Life isn't always fun and games. It can often be tough, and when everything feels a bit too much, it can be hard to make the choice to **focus on what's good.** But even then, it's still a choice we get to make for ourselves.

With a brain that has been **trained through practice,** we can always find a way to be grateful. And when we are thankful, it always leads to **greater happiness** in our lives.

So, when times are tough, choose to look at the positive. Seek out the good stuff and remember your blessings. How you deal with life—both the good and the bad—**is your choice.**

Together, let's live full of gratitude. **For life, for friends, for family,** for whatever it is that is good in your life. After all, they are gifts. **And it is always good to say thank you for presents.**

CHAPTER 9

YOUR

PASSION

CAN BRING INCREDIBLE REWARDS

When I was a young teenager at school, I experienced some bullying. There was an older boy who liked to **blow a foghorn** to let us younger boys know that he was on the lookout for someone to beat up. **Me and my friend once hid in a cupboard to escape him.** It didn't work. He found us, and then we both got thrown around pretty nastily.

(You'll get why I'm telling you this story in a moment, but before I do, I just want to remind you that if you are going through bullying, **the best, bravest, and smartest thing** to do is to go straight to a trusted adult and tell them what's happening to you. There is help out there if you look and ask, **and you are never alone.)**

Anyway, back to the **foghorn and the cupboard.** The bullying was difficult at the time, but it also led me to something incredible and positive that has been a **guiding light** in my life ever since.

AS SOON AS I COULD, I JOINED THE MARTIAL ARTS CLUB AT SCHOOL.

It started off as a way to learn to **defend myself** from the foghorn bully, but before long, I realized that I had found **something that I loved** and that I wanted to try to master.

STICK AT IT!

The great thing about our passions is that if we give them our time and dedication, **rewards will always come our way.**

My passion as a teenager was karate. I loved how it was more about defeating your opponent **by being calm and smart** rather than simply using brute force. Mastering technique and being familiar with difficult situations was the aim.

AND, OF COURSE, IT WAS A TOUGH PHYSICAL CHALLENGE,

WHICH WAS FUN!

One of the classes was always held on Sunday evening, and that one was the **hardest class to get motivated to go to.** It was always dark and cold, and I didn't always feel in the mood to go out and practice punching. **Sunday evenings felt like time to relax.** That was what all my school friends were doing: chilling out and watching TV. **But I kept going.** I made the decision to go to the difficult classes, even when I didn't always feel like it. Invariably, once I was there, I loved it!

My first **big reward** came when I was selected to go on tour to Japan with the Karate Union of Great Britain. While there, I had some amazing experiences. Not only did I get to spend time in remote parts of Japan, high up in the mountains, that most tourists never see, but I was also lucky enough to train with one of the most revered karate grandmasters of all time: **Sensei Yahara.** Not bad for a skinny kid from England who, not long before that, was hiding in a cupboard to protect himself from a bully!

I am so glad I went to those Sunday evening classes after all.

CALM IN THE STORM

After three years of dedication, hard work, **and a few black eyes,** I finally earned my karate black belt. Eventually, **I became one of the youngest** second dan black belts in the UK—which is one rank above a black belt—

ALL WHILE STILL AT SCHOOL.

While **reaching our goals** is always fun, the most important part of all this karate was that I was learning qualities that were going to serve me well in the adventures that **I hadn't even yet dreamed would come my way in life.** Like learning to be calm in the storm and how not to panic.

Karate is all about this and facing our fears. Having a calm attitude in the face of scary situations—a real storm, for example—is one of the key character traits an adventurer can have. I have to use that skill all the time. **And karate helped build that in me.** Because one passion can help fuel others.

The thing about having a passion is that you will often have to make difficult choices. You might have to turn down doing other fun things in order to practice and improve in what it is you love. But you never know the exciting places those passions might lead you and what doors they might open.

SO, GO FOR
THINGS, TRAIN
HARD, DO
YOUR BEST, BE
COMMITTED,
AND NEVER
GIVE UP. YOU
NEVER KNOW
JUST WHERE
IT MIGHT
LEAD YOU...

CHAPTER 10

HANDLING FAILURE AND

BOUNCING BACK FROM IT

When I decided to try out for the **British Special Forces'** 21 SAS Regiment, I wasn't sure whether I would be able to manage it. Around nine in ten people who attempt selection for this super-specialist, elite branch of the military fail to get in. **Nine in ten.** That number feels like a scarily high rate of rejection, right? I didn't know whether I was going to be one of the nine who failed or the one who got in. It's the great unknown.

BUT ONE THING I DID KNOW WAS THAT IF I DIDN'T TRY, I'D NEVER KNOW.

So I said to myself: "I'm going to **give it my best,** give it my everything, and just go for it!" And if I didn't make it, well, at least it wouldn't be for a lack of trying.

That's not to say that I always thought that I would get in. I didn't. I had many doubts. In fact, doubt did its best to put me off at every turn. Doubt is always going to be part of any big goal we set for ourselves. But that's OK. **Our job is to tune it out and keep going.**

MASTER YOUR MIND

First up on the journey to attempting SAS Selection, I had to get fit. Seriously fit.

Fitness didn't come as naturally to me as it did to some of my friends. I had to work really hard at it. I definitely wasn't ripped with muscles like some of the other guys going for Selection.

What I did have, though, was a quiet determination and an inner fight. (It's something I believe that we all have in us—you included.) Selection puts its hopefuls through a complete beasting. That's why it's the most elite fighting force in the world.

I can't tell you too many details, because a lot of the Selection tests have to stay secret. But what I can let you in on is that it involves an enormous amount of hard work and physical exhaustion. **And what about the mind?** Well, that's an even tougher battle for every soldier attempting to join the SAS.

There's a lot of hill running and push-ups, and a lot of long marches across the high Welsh mountains, often in deep snow, at night, while carrying a really heavy backpack. (Imagine giving a friend a piggyback ride for many hours uphill.) There are also the times when you have to navigate tight underground tunnels in the pitch dark while trying not to give in to terror and panic.

I often vomited as a result of what we were putting our bodies through. The skin on our back and feet was sometimes rubbed raw and bleeding from the weight of our packs and the blisters from our boots. One of my best buddies, Trucker, even had to march on through the pain of two broken big toes. **Broken from the pounding his feet had taken on one particularly long, hard march.**

While my body was being pushed to its limits, I had to work especially hard to not let the doubts bring me down. All of us on Selection had to master that. It was the will inside us that made us get back up, haul on our packs

 again, bandage our blisters, and carry on. Because as you know, worthwhile things take grit, effort, and perseverance. And failure.

FAILING CAN HURT

On my first attempt at passing Selection, after putting myself through so much, I was failed. Off the course. I had taken too long to complete a march.

I'm not ashamed to say that there were tears. **I was totally exhausted.** I'd worked so hard, endured so much pain, spent every little drop of determination and fight I had in me to try to make it into the SAS. I'd pushed my body, and I'd pushed my mind. Yet still, here I was, rejected.

I felt low and so upset. The only light at the end of the dark tunnel was that the SAS selectors had offered me the chance to try again. They didn't offer that to every soldier who failed.

THAT INVITATION FROM THE SELECTORS SPARKED A FLICKER OF HOPE.

It was now time to replace any doubt with renewed hope, fear with courage, self-pity with pride. **So, I tried again** and went through the entire 21 SAS Selection process once more.

AND THIS TIME, FINALLY, I MADE IT THROUGH.

FAILING CAN BE WINNING

When you succeed at something, it sort of swallows up the failure that might have come first. But we should remember how important it is to fail, because the truth is that, often, **success isn't possible without some sort of failure**—and sometimes quite a lot of it.

If you piled up all the failures I've experienced in my life, it'd make quite a mountain. **And I'm proud of that.** Those failures are the stepping stones we must use to get to the **good stuff.**

Sure, it's never much fun when we fail, **but going through failure is key.** And the failures always make us stronger. Like when I gave Selection another go. **I was stronger and smarter the second time around.** I learned that when others were giving up, I had it in me to give a little bit more.

There's no shame in failing. It shows that you've had the courage to try in the first place, and you should always **be proud of that.**

Like the SAS motto says: **"Who Dares, Wins."** My question to you is: Can you dare to fail? Maybe it'll be once. Maybe twice. Maybe 20 times. But can you **still dare to get up** and give it one more go?

Because if you can do that, then you can do anything. **As someone once told me:**

"THERE'S ONLY REALLY ONE FAILURE: WHEN WE GIVE UP."

CHAPTER 11

BE
PREPARED!

You might have heard the motto **"be prepared."** If you're one of the 57 million Scouts in the world, then you definitely have, because it's been a fundamental principle of the Scouts since Scouting started. As **chief scout**, doing my best to be prepared is **something that's really helped me in my life.**

Being prepared is about being ready for anything that might come along. It might be about having the right equipment to help you get out of a tough situation. If I go out on an adventure without checking the batteries in my headlamp or packing the **anti-venom for snake bites,** it could have some potentially life-threatening consequences.

Being prepared might simply be about **packing smart** for a trip away. Or it might be about prepping yourself for something that's going to challenge your body or your brain. **Either way, it's about readying yourself in the best way you can.**

It doesn't necessarily mean that you'll always succeed, but you're giving yourself the best possible chance to.

BEING PREPARED IS ABOUT BEING ON THE FRONT FOOT, READY FOR ACTION.

MIND GAMES

Chess grandmasters are **super-skilled** at seeing four, five, or sometimes even 10 moves ahead on the board. They are **mentally prepared** for what their opponent might do and what they will then do themselves to win.

What's ahead that you might need to prepare yourself for? Maybe an exam or a sports event? **How can you prepare best?** It might be as simple as knowing some facts on key topics that are likely to come up in an exam. It might be doing some sprinting in the garden to get faster in the weeks before your school sports day. That's you getting prepared. **You're giving yourself the best shot at being able to achieve your goals.**

PRACTICE=PREPARED

An athlete from a cold country would be bold to turn up at a hot summer tournament without first doing some training in the heat, right? Instead, they will want to **prepare their body** so they'll be as ready as they can be to compete for that gold medal. Everyone wants to win, but not everyone has the determination to do the training. **And generally, the rewards go to those who give the most and train the hardest.**

I like the quote: **"The will to win means nothing without the will to train."**

This doesn't just work for athletes. **Want to play for the school soccer team?** Practice dribbling the ball around obstacles so you can dodge other players on the field.

Got an audition for a dance show? Rehearse the routine more than anyone else. **Your body will learn exactly which step comes next, and then you will do it brilliantly**, even with lots of people watching.

Practice makes perfect. You have to put in the hard work to get the good results. And the more you practice, the better you will get. **Simple.**

VISUALIZE IT!

There's a **cool technique** that will definitely help you be prepared in both your body **AND** in your mind.

IT'S CALLED VISUALIZATION,

and lots of top athletes use it as part of their training.

I use it all the time before **big climbs**, giving talks, or doing TV work.

In visualization, you picture yourself in your head doing the thing you're about to do. **Where will you be? What will be around you?** Think of the sounds, the smells, and the people you will see. Now, go through the task in your head and make sure that it goes just as you hope from start to finish. If you're a gymnast, visualize the perfect routine that will get you the best score from the judges. Maybe you're a skateboarder. **Run a short movie in your mind** of you executing the perfect kickflip.

AND THEN
DO IT AGAIN
AND AGAIN.

What's happening in the brain when you visualize is AMAZING. It's basically the same as if you were doing the action with your body, only you're not moving. And we already know that the more we do something, the better we get at it. You can prepare your performance with your mind in the same way as your body. **And it works.**

SLEEP IS MAGIC

There are some simple and obvious ways **to be prepared for life.** Do difficult things. Listen more than you speak. Be kind. Eat natural foods. **Be outside lots.**

But one that is often overlooked is getting enough sleep. I've slept in some pretty wild places before, like inside a dead camel carcass in the **Sahara Desert.** I know how important sleep can be. And I also know how difficult things can be when you fail to get enough sleep for long periods of time.

Going to sleep early is like a **magic formula** when it comes to preparing ourselves for success. When we sleep, we give both our body and our mind the best chance to repair themselves. Then, we can start the next day refreshed and raring to go. **It's like recharging our own batteries!**

Whether you're a Scout or not, you already have everything you need to be **prepared for life** and for *adventure.* It's inside you! Be the person who thinks ahead, who's not too lazy to practice, and who keeps themselves as healthy as they can.

TIME SPENT PREPARING IS NEVER WASTED.

CHAPTER 12

THE POWER

OF
POSITIVITY

Here is some good news:
Every day, we get to choose a positive attitude.

And here is the bad news: It isn't always easy. We all know that **having a positive attitude makes life brighter, easier, and more fun.** But some days we might not feel either positive or strong. And that's OK. It doesn't mean that we can't try our best to choose how we approach the day.

Are we going to do our best to be positive and kind? Or will we let negative feelings dictate how the day will go? **We decide.**

What I have learned is that **the more we practice** being positive, brave, kind, and resilient, **the easier it becomes** to choose those qualities every day.

Being positive instead of negative **is a choice.** To be kind is a choice. How we act, what we say, and the attitudes we have are all choices. We really can decide how we tackle every day. **Pretty cool, right?**

Positivity is a key value for adventurers but also for anyone who wants to live the best life they can. It adds a finishing touch of sparkle to everything we do. *And life always needs some extra sparkle.*

SMALL STEPS

I definitely lost a bit of my sparkle when I was in the hospital recovering from breaking my back. It was a really difficult time for me. **Choosing positivity was hard** when I was in pain, unsure about the future, and scared of whether I'd ever fully recover. And I didn't always manage it.

But there was always a new day to try again. A new day to start over and try to choose positivity. And eventually, that choice got easier to make. **It also made my days better.** So, I kept trying to choose to be optimistic and full of hope. I started to make plans and set goals. Even if right then, those goals seemed a long way away.

Small steps were the key. Conscious decisions every day to do my best and to be positive and kind. And soon enough, those **small steps become big journeys** that can define our lives.

WORDS MATTER

How we talk to ourselves and about ourselves really matters. There's something called "self-talk," and it is basically the voice inside our heads.

Self-talk can be positive or negative. Again, we have a choice to make here. We can either speak to ourselves using positive words or using negative ones. Maybe think about how we would talk to a friend. **We'd cheer a friend on.** We'd tell them that we think that they're great and that they can do it!

We should be talking to ourselves in the same way. Next time you catch that voice in your head telling you something negative about yourself—like you can't do it or you're not as good as someone else—stop and change it. Try not to let negative thoughts enter your precious heart.

Our inner voice wants to help us, but it takes direction from what we allow it to say. If the voice isn't helping, **then change the words.** With practice, we can all do that, and we can ensure that our inner chats are encouraging and uplifting.

Practice it a bit today before you tackle a task. It might feel strange at first, **but persevere**, and make positive, kind self-talk a part of who you are.

PRIME MINISTERS AND THUNDERSTORMS

There's one adventure I remember where my **positivity and optimism** were really tested.

I had been asked to take the prime minister of India on an adventure into the wild for TV. Weeks of planning had gone into this **expedition**. The crew and I were ready, and we were pumped to be filming with a global head of state. We had done a show like this once before with the US president, and all had gone smoothly. **What could possibly go wrong here?** The answer was a lot!

Firstly, nature decided to throw us a curveball in the shape of an **enormous storm**. The prime minister's helicopter couldn't land where we'd planned in the rainforest. Instead, we had to race down river and put him and his **Secret Service** in small boats. But the boats were overloaded, and water was coming over the sides. It was starting to look like they might actually sink.

Everyone was soon soaking wet, behind schedule, and potentially in danger. **Many in the Indian team were suggesting that we abort.**

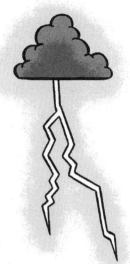

The motto of the Royal Marines Commandos is: **"cheerfulness in the face of adversity."** That means that when times are tough, do your best to be upbeat and positive. **You come alive in a crisis.**

All the team did this! They worked twice as hard, **solved problems,** encouraged those who were cold and wet, and shared clothes and supplies, and we adapted our plan on the go. All in all, we pulled off the impossible and **filmed an epic journey** with the prime minister of India.

No one knew how close we had been to having it fall through, and it was only because of the team's **relentless positivity** that we achieved it.

WHEN WE ACTIVELY CHOOSE TO HAVE A GREAT ATTITUDE, WE CAN ACHIEVE AMAZING THINGS.

ENTHUSIASTIC ENERGY

Enthusiasm is positivity in action. **When you're really fired up** and excited about something, it's infectious. Other people will catch a whiff of your enthusiasm and want some of it for themselves. After all, would you rather hang around with people who are a bit **"whatever"** about stuff and who aren't that bothered? Or the people who are **REALLY** excited about things and make things happen?

Like positivity, **there's nothing stopping us** from choosing to be enthusiastic about what's going on in our lives. We can be those **enthusiastic people** who others want to hang around with! Or we can be the alternative: downbeat, boring, and bored. But that doesn't sound like fun for anyone!

My dad once said to me: **"If you can be the most enthusiastic person you know, then you won't go too far wrong."** He was right. We might never be able to be the fastest, or cleverest, or strongest of the people around us, but there is nothing stopping us from being the **most positive and the most enthusiastic.** It's a decision. And true champions choose those attitudes every day.

CHAPTER 13

LOOK OUT FOR FUN,

BUT KNOW WHEN TO GET TOUGH

My experiences in the wild have, at times, been quite **dangerous** and often truly scary. The danger goes hand-in-hand with always making sure that, as a team, we are as safe as possible. The people who film alongside me are incredible at their job of operating the cameras but also at doing it safely. That's a great skill and is such a vital part of our role together. **We've got to stay alive for the next adventure.**

Something else that's **really important** is to have as much fun as possible on our adventures—not only in the wild but also in life. **After all, adventures can be full of rough patches.** But if you mope and moan about the tough stuff, it never changes anything or makes it any better. It simply makes the situation worse for everyone.

That's why I always try to make a conscious decision to **smile when it is raining** and to keep fun, laughter, and positivity at the heart of all I do. After all,

we are so lucky to get to live on this amazing Earth. Life is the ultimate gift. **Let's never waste it by being grumpy and negative.** That's the ultimate ungratefulness.

AS CHAMPIONS AND ADVENTURERS, WE CHOOSE TO LIVE DIFFERENTLY. A BETTER, MORE UPBEAT WAY. IT IS WHAT SETS US APART.

A STATE OF MIND

Are you being forced out for a family walk on a wet and windy day when **all you want to do is hide under your duvet?**

Well, if you're going to go on the walk, why not make it as fun as possible?! **Maybe a wet walk simply means bigger puddles to splash in with your buddies!** After all, mud and water—with a hot cocoa at the end when you get home—are some of the **greatest** things in life!

It's up to you to decide to seek out and create the fun in life. **It's all a state of mind.**

PRACTICAL JOKER

The importance of looking for fun was something I learned from my dad when I was a kid. Dad was a big fan of practical jokes. I'd often get roped into helping him with them, even though it would sometimes **get me in trouble** with my family.

One time, we stretched plastic wrap over my aunt and uncle's toilet seat. I can still remember my aunt's **squeal** when she went for a pee! But life is all about creating great memories that make you laugh for many years. Just make sure that the jokes aren't unkind, **and be sensitive to people.**

(By the way, I've **apologized** to my aunt so many times over the years for my part in that joke. It was maybe pushing it a bit far!)

KNOW WHEN TO GET SERIOUS

The wise people in life know when to have fun and joke around and **when to be serious and focused.** It might be for safety reasons or for some important tests to become a doctor or a climbing instructor. Those critical moments deserve your total focus and respect. Know when to play and when to work.

My dad somehow knew when it was time to stop fooling around. He had been a Royal Marines commando—an elite part of the Royal Navy—so I figure he was trained to find the **balance between looking for fun and taking things seriously.** I've always tried to have that balance too.

He helped me see that it was good to be the person who can play the fool but is tough and reliable with **the things that really matter.**

PLAYING PING-PONG HALFWAY UP A MOUNTAIN

One **adventure** really sticks in my mind where I applied what Dad taught me.

I'd taken Roger Federer—**one of the world's greatest tennis players**—out on an expedition in the Swiss Alps. It was freezing, the terrain was gnarly, and Roger had already had to dig deep when we shared a **dead fish's eyeball** as a source of fluids and nutrition. (He said that he felt it pop in his mouth!)

Then—even though it was seriously cold and we were halfway up a **really big mountain**—we stopped for a game of mini ping-pong using a tiny fold-up table I had put in my **backpack**.

As well as putting our **minds and bodies** to the test in the wild, I thought that it would be fun to have this moment as a little pick-me-up at a *tough moment on the journey.*

As **Roger Federer** balanced precariously on the snowy ridge in the mountain forest, I set up the mini table on the ice. **We both ended up laughing out loud** as we bopped the tiny

ball backward and forward across the tiny net. I got totally thrashed by him—of course!—**but it was so fun.**

Then it was time to **get focused** and work hard again. We had one final and treacherous ascent to tackle before we **reached the summit.**

We both knew that it was not the time for laughs anymore. When you're climbing, **your life's on the line,** and you can't mess around. We ascended that final mountain and reached safety. **But the highlight for me had actually been the ping-pong match in the wild!**

STAY ALERT

How good would you say you are at knowing when to stop joking and start knuckling down? It involves being alert and tuned in to your surroundings. Reading a situation like a pro. Thinking about what's ahead and how others might be feeling.

So, try to be that person who always brings fun and joy to a situation. But also be smart enough to know when to take important things seriously and tackle the job ahead with focus.

IT'S A TOUGH BALANCE TO FIND, AND WE WON'T ALWAYS GET IT RIGHT.

But remember—the more we practice, the better we will get.

CHAPTER 14

NAVIGATING

FRIENDSHIPS

Besties, pals, bros, buddies... whatever we call them, our friends are the family we choose. We might have a tight group of just a few or a whole team of people **we like to spend our time with,** but no matter what our friendships look like,

WE SHOULD ALWAYS TRY TO BE THE BEST FRIEND WE POSSIBLY CAN TO OTHERS.

MY BRILLIANT BUDDIES

I'm super-proud to have incredible buddies in my life, some of whom I've known for as long as I can remember. **Mick—who you met in chapter eight—**has been a close friend since we were kids growing up together. We went to the same school, where we both started climbing, and since then, we have

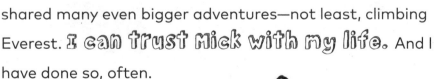

shared many even bigger adventures—not least, climbing Everest. **I can trust Mick with my life.** And I have done so, often.

Another buddy, Rupert, **I train with almost every day,** lifting weights and playing sports. We live near each other, we work together side by side, and we swim in rivers whenever we can. I can tell Rupert anything, and he shares all his struggles and triumphs with me as well. **We always build each other up.** And the best part is that his grandfather and Shara's grandfather were best friends too!

And then there's Charlie, who you might know because he wrote a smash-hit book called *The Boy, The Mole, The Fox, and The Horse.* Charlie might be well-known now, but we have been best buddies since I was a teenager, and we would hang upside down in trees, "forget" to shower, sleep outside whenever we could, and generally get into mischief. **Once, we even rowed down the River Thames in London in a bathtub for charity.** Charlie is kind, and fun, and loyal, and we still hang out as much as we possibly can.

Then, there is Trucker—*my buddy from the Special Forces*—and then Gilo, Hugo, and Al.

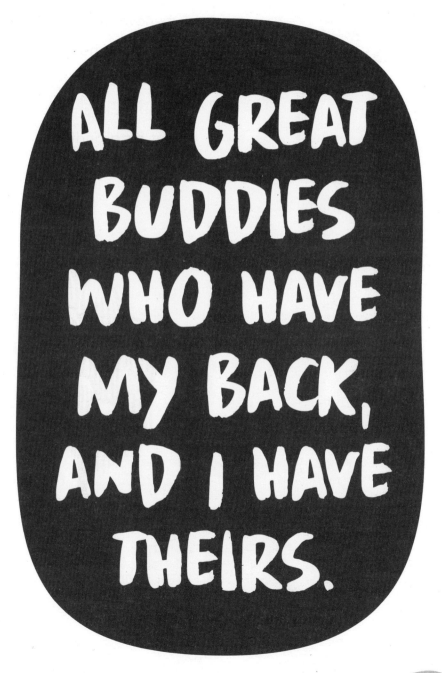

ALL GREAT BUDDIES WHO HAVE MY BACK, AND I HAVE THEIRS.

FRIENDSHIPS AS DIFFERENT AS WE ARE

The point of telling you about my best friends is to show you that **one friendship can look really different than another,** and they can all provide so many different things. After all, us human beings are pretty diverse, so it makes sense that our friendships will be diverse too.

There doesn't need to be a one-size-fits-all when it comes to friends. They are all unique, and they are all special. And when it comes to things of value, you've got to **look after them and nurture them.** That way, the friendships endure and get even stronger.

WE ARE THE COMPANY WE KEEP

What does matter is how your friendships make you feel. It's possible to tell a lot about someone by the friends they choose to have around them. Whoever said "*your vibe attracts your tribe*" was right! We tend to become like the people we hang out with—*it's basic human nature.*

If we want to be friends with people **who will encourage us,** laugh with us, **cry with us,** keep our secrets, **never judge us,** and make us feel good about ourselves, **then we have to be all of those things to others first.**

As the quote says:

"SHOW ME YOUR FRIENDS, AND I WILL SHOW YOU YOUR FUTURE."

You might have **friends you play sports with,** and others you know from a youth club or a faith group. Maybe you're BFFs with your neighbor or **the person on the next desk at school.**

whatever our friendships look like, the most important thing **we should remember** is this:

TO HAVE A GREAT FRIEND, FIRST BE A GREAT FRIEND.

CHAPTER 15

IT'S NOT
ALL ABOUT

A

GRADES

I most definitely wasn't a straight-A kind of student when I was at school. In fact, my teacher once wrote in my end-of-year report that I "lacked all sense of purpose." I'd see other boys effortlessly coasting to their top-of-the-class positions and straight-A grades. Meanwhile, I'd discover that I'd failed math... again.

When the letter containing my GCSE exam results landed on the doormat back home on the Isle of Wight, I remember intercepting it and sprinting to my favorite tree right at the bottom of our garden. It was a lofty sycamore with branches perfect for a challenging climb, and once I'd monkeyed my way to the very top, I would look out at a view across our village.

On that results day, the far-reaching view from up there helped me keep whatever might be lurking in that envelope in perspective.

I NEEDED TIME TO TAKE A BREATH, LOOK OUT ON THE BIG WIDE WORLD, AND REMIND MYSELF THAT LIFE IS ABOUT SO MUCH MORE THAN THE NUMBERS OR LETTERS ON A REPORT CARD.

DIRECTION AND EFFORT TRUMPS ALL

If our grades aren't perfect—or even particularly good—just remember that not being "**classroom clever**" doesn't mean that we should write ourselves off as being stupid or a failure. I was really clever when I was out in the wild, **listening to the rhythms of nature,** thinking on my feet, and using my brain and muscles together to help me stay safe when I climbed or went out on the sea.

Of course, **I'm not saying results don't matter.** I'm just saying that they don't define you. As long as we have done our best to prepare ourselves for the test, or given proper attention to the assignment, **we have done right by ourselves,** and that is something we can be proud of.

LIFE IS MAINLY ABOUT EFFORT AND FOCUS.

If you have an upward trajectory, **that's all that matters,** even if you start from last place. And our worth as a human being most definitely should not be tied to exam results or school achievements.

HOW CAN WE GROW IF EVERYTHING COMES EASY?

Let me share with you something **I believe to be true...**

The great successes in life are rarely the people who don't have to work hard to get perfect grades. **I'll say it again:**

THE GREAT SUCCESSES IN LIFE ARE RARELY THE PEOPLE WHO DON'T HAVE TO WORK HARD TO GET PERFECT GRADES!

If top grades or sports trophies are won without effort, then we can miss out on important lessons. It is the effort and persistence—whatever they are toward—**that help us grow and improve** as humans.

It's all those cool things we've been talking about together in this book. Like learning to deal with failure. **Like how we mustn't allow fear to hold us back.** Like how life can offer up the most amazing things if we aren't afraid of taking risks and giving our all. Like the importance of following our hearts and **knowing the power of true friends.** These are things that we are rarely taught at school.

I was really lucky to have parents who believed that the most important thing was to **follow our dreams** while being good to people in our lives along the way. **They never once scolded me for failing.**

Not having to be afraid of what might happen if I did fail at something—at math, or trying to get a karate black belt, or anything else I did as a kid—**gave me the freedom** to take risks in my life, and I am forever grateful for that.

MAYBE YOUR PARENTS OR CAREGIVERS THINK THE SAME AS MINE DID, OR MAYBE THEY DON'T—EVERYONE WILL BE DIFFERENT. BUT EITHER WAY, YOU CAN CHOOSE HOW YOU THINK ABOUT THIS.

It might not feel like it now, but I promise that school will not be your summit moment. There will be **so many more amazing things** to come in your life.

If you're having a horrible time of it right now, **hang on in there.** Be proud that you're hanging tight, and keep being true to yourself by doing your best. And if school is a great place to be and you're working hard and getting top grades, good for you. But remember to **be most proud of your effort,** not just your grades.

And **always** try to be kind and gentle. Because as the saying goes: "**Be humble, or you'll stumble!**"

ABOVE ALL, KNOW THAT YOU ARE ALWAYS MORE THAN THE GRADES ON A PIECE OF PAPER.

So, my **fellow adventurer,** your gear bag is hopefully now bulging with **life-enhancing,** helpful equipment! It has been great to journey with you as a team, but now it's time to hand the map and the compass to you... **you ready?!**

Together, we've explored **determination,** kindness, **friendship,** always doing our best, **confidence,** grit, **learning to fail,** positivity, **the importance of gratitude,** how to take risks, and—of course—that all-important **NGU (Never Give Up)** spirit. **Phew!**

Remember that **life is a journey,** not a destination. We're always learning, always growing, and always trying to do better. **That's the key.**

I'll still be on my journey, just as you'll always be on yours. But let's always stay friends and help each other if we ever need it. **That's so important.**

So **let's get out there** and make that journey EPIC!

You Vs The World? **Yep, you've got this!**

Senior Editor Tori Kosara
Editor Vicky Armstrong
Senior Designer Nathan Martin
Production Editor Siu Yin Chan
Senior Production Controller Louise Minihane
Senior Acquisitions Editor Katy Flint
Managing Art Editor Vicky Short
Publishing Director Mark Searle

Acknowledgments
DK would like to thank Emma Roberts for her editorial
consultancy; Heather Wilcox and Lori Hand for proofreading;
the team at Bear Grylls Ventures; Caroline Michel,
Kieron Fairweather, and Francesca Morgan
at Peters Fraser + Dunlop

First American Edition, 2023
Published in the United States by DK Publishing
1745 Broadway, 20th Floor, New York, NY 10019

Page design copyright © 2023 Dorling Kindersley Limited
DK, a Division of Penguin Random House LLC
23 24 25 26 27 10 9 8 7 6 5 4 3 2
006–333375–April/23

Text copyright © BGV Global Limited, 2023
Illustrations copyright © Jason Ford, 2023

A catalog record for this book is available from the Library of Congress.
ISBN: 978-0-7440-7067-5

DK books are available at special discounts when purchased in bulk for sales
promotions, premiums, fund-raising, or educational use.
For details, contact: DK Publishing Special Markets,
1745 Broadway, 20th Floor, New York, NY 10019
SpecialSales@dk.com

Printed and bound in Great Britain

For the curious
www.dk.com